# Adults and Bullying

## Keeping Adults Safe In Families and Communities

written by Terry Hitchcock
illustrated by Laurie Barrows

Text © 2018 Terry Hitchcock
Terryhitchcock@gmail.com
TerryHitchcock.com

Illustrations © 2018 Laurie Barrows
"Making the World a Happier Place,
One Smile at a Time" ™
LaurieBarrows@att.net
LaurieBarrows.com

ISBN 13: 978-1-7321520-3-8

Printed in the United States of America

Published in the United States of America

*dedicated to our children -*
*Jason Hitchcock*
*Christian Hitchcock*
*Teri Sue Hitchcock*
*Kim Schneewind*

The subject of bullying is an issue for our adults, whatever age. This book is focused on our adults (The companion book focuses on *Children and Bullying*).

Adult bullies operate in a set pattern. They are not interested in working things out. They are not interested in compromise. Adult bullies are only interested in power and domination.

## What is bullying?

Bullying is unwanted, aggressive behavior. Bullying can affect anyone. Adults who are bullied and who bully others may have serious, lasting problems over one's lifetime.

# Types of bullying

## Social bullying

This involves damaging a person's reputation or relationships and includes:
Spreading rumors about someone
Leaving someone out on purpose
Telling other adults and children not to be friends with someone
Embarrassing someone in public

Verbal bullying includes saying or writing mean things and includes:
Name-calling
Taunting
Teasing
Inappropriate sexual comments
Threatening to cause harm

Physical bullying involves hurting a person's body or possessions and includes:
Tripping and pushing
Making mean or rude hand gestures
Hitting, kicking and pinching
Spitting
Taking or breaking someone's things

**When and where bullying happens**

Bullying can occur anywhere. It can happen at home, in the neighborhood, or on the Internet.

## Who is at risk?

Bullying can happen anywhere: cities; suburbs; or rural towns. Depending on the environment, some groups; such as lesbian, gay, bisexual, transgender, adults with disabilities, and socially isolated adults; may be at an increased risk of being bullied.

## Effects of bullying

Bullying can affect everyone—those who are bullied, those who bully, and those who witness bullying. Bullying is linked to many negative outcomes including impacts on mental health, substance use, and suicide. It is important to talk to adults to determine whether bullying, or something else, is a concern.

## Race, religion and diversity

Communities that respect diversity can help protect adults against bullying behavior. However, when adults perceived as different are not in supportive environments, they may be at a higher risk of being bullied.

Disability and special needs
Adults with disabilities; such as physical, developmental, intellectual, emotional, and sensory disabilities; are at an increased risk of being bullied. Any number of factors; physical vulnerability, social skill challenges, or intolerant environments may increase the risk.

Adults with special health needs, such as epilepsy or food allergies, also may be at higher risk of being bullied. Bullying can include making fun of adults because of their allergies or exposing them to the things they are allergic to. In these cases, bullying is not just serious, it can mean life or death.

# Cyber bullying

Cyber bullying is bullying that takes place over digital devices like cell phones, computers, and tablets. Cyber bullying includes sending, posting, or sharing negative, harmful, false, or mean content about someone else. It can include sharing personal or private information about someone else causing embarrassment or humiliation. Some cyber bullying crosses the line into unlawful or criminal behavior.

27 percent were called offensive names
22 percent had someone try to purposefully embarrass them
8 percent were physically threatened
8 percent were stalked
7 percent were harassed for a sustained period
6 percent were sexually harassed

# How to prevent bullying

Communities, families and other caring adults have a role to play in preventing bullying. They can:
• Talk about what bullying is and how to stand up to it safely. Tell adults bullying is unacceptable. Make sure adults know how to get help.
• Check in with adults often. Listen to them. Know their friends, ask and understand their concerns.
• Encourage adults to do what they love. Special activities, interests, and hobbies can boost confidence, help adults make friends, and protect them from bullying behavior.
• Model with kindness and respect.

# Notes, Ideas & Actions

# Notes, Ideas & Actions

# Notes, Ideas & Actions

# Notes, Ideas & Actions

# Notes, Ideas & Actions

# Notes, Ideas & Actions

# Notes, Ideas & Actions

# Notes, Ideas & Actions

# ABOUT THE AUTHOR

In 1996, Terry ran for children, the equivalent of a marathon or more each day for 75 consecutive days, arriving at the Opening Ceremonies of the Summer Olympics. He knew that his banner to carry for life was to honor our future, our children. From that point, Terry speaks all over the country to benefit our children.

This book, *Adults and Bullying,* is an important topic that has destroyed or taken away precious lives each day in our adult communities. We don't talk about it and many don't recognize it happening. It is.

His first successful book, *American Business: The Last Hurrah?* tells the story of our country's successes and failures in 1984. One of his recent books, *A Father's Odyssey,* received the prestigious DOVE Award and now is read in over 27 countries. Hollywood produced a successful documentary of part of Terry's life called MY RUN and now a feature film, Pushing Life, is planned for production.

Terry and his wife Jean reside in Clearwater, Florida

TerryHitchcock.com
TerryHitchcock@gmail.com

# ABOUT THE ILLUSTRATOR

## MISSION STATEMENT:
"Making the World A Happier Place, One Smile at a Time."™

"Art should be fun!" states illustrator Laurie Barrows. The artist's work sparkles with playfulness. Her positive approach to life shines through. Bright color celebrates the joy the artist finds in her subject.
This is her 222nd book

"I carry my philosophy of life into my work. I believe in a positive attitude and the power of love," says Barrows, "My goal with children's art is to touch lives with the wonderful luxury of innocence by creating positive images for the young."

"Children need a positive and empowering environment in which to grow and flourish. Children need freedom to dream. Everyday should be a celebration of joy and wonder. Developing a sense of self through play fosters creativity, imagination, and problem solving. We can all benefit by returning to a simpler time, if only for a moment."

"Success has many definitions. If my work makes you smile, and brightens your day, I've been successful."

LaurieBarrows.com
LaurieBarrows@att.net

**RECOMMENDED READING:**

**Living Beyond Impossible ~ The Terry Hitchcock Story**

By

Ronald Joseph Kule

Foreword by Tracy Repchuk

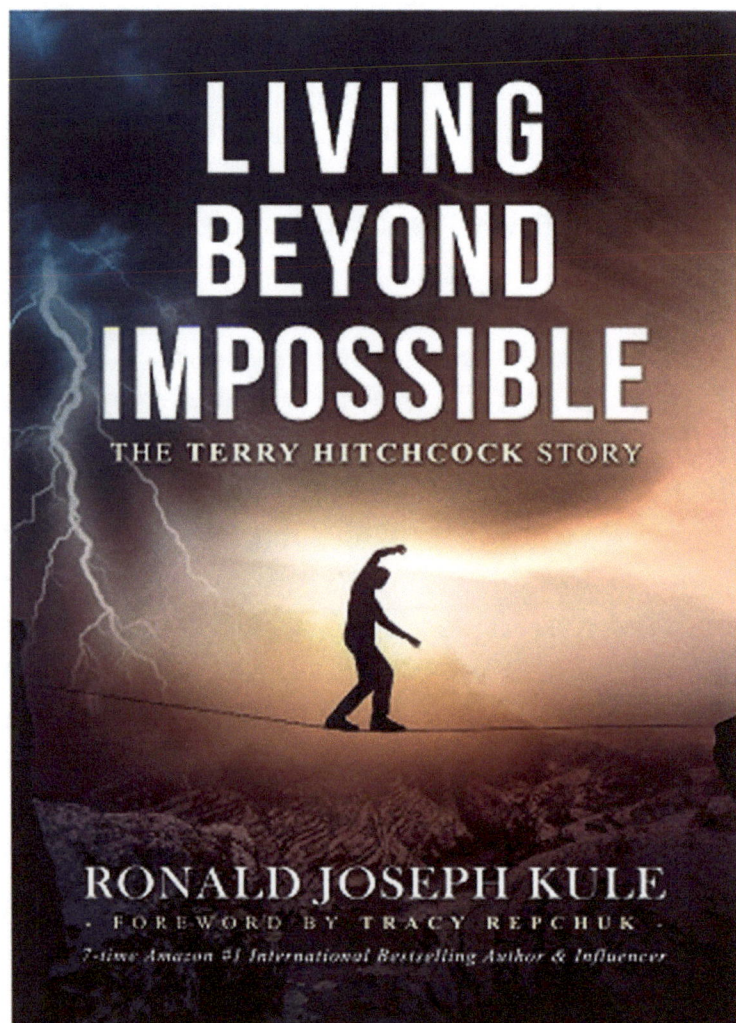

*335 pages, softcover & Kindle book formats*

For signed copies, order through:

https://RonKuleBooks.com

www.ingramcontent.com/pod-product-compliance
Lightning Source LLC
Chambersburg PA
CBHW041806040426
42448CB00005B/295